©2021 by Reginal Jackson
ALL RIGHTS RESERVED

No part of this book may be used or reproduced by any means: graphic, electronic, or mechanical, including photocopying, recording, taping or by any information storage retrieval system without the written permission of the author except in the case of brief quotations embodied in critical articles and reviews. Because of the dynamic nature of the Internet, any web addresses or links contained in this book may have changed since publication and may no longer be valid. Although every precaution has been taken to verify the accuracy of the information contained herein, the author and publisher assume no responsibility for any errors or omissions so that no liability is assumed for damages that may result from the use of information contained within. The views expressed in this work are solely those of the author and do not necessarily reflect the views of the publisher whereby the publisher hereby disclaims any responsibility for them.

Traitmarker Books
2984 Del Rio Pike
Franklin, TN 37069
www.traitmarkerbooks.com
traitmarker@gmail.com

Interior Text Font: Minion Pro
Interior Title Fonts: Minion Pro
Editor: Robbie Grayson
Illustrator: Irfan Budi

ISBN 978-1-08797-619-8

Printed in the United States of America

The Sports Kids
Crime Fighters
The Out-of-Towners

Written by Reginal Jackson
Illustrated by Irfan Budi
Traitmarker Books

I dedicate this book to my beautiful wife, Tina Jackson, for always encouraging me to make my dreams a reality. To put on paper the things I imagine for the world to see. I also dedicate this book to my awesome children who all have been a blessing in my life.

The school bell rang and the kids excitedly ran out of the classroom doors.

"Wait up guys?" Jujy yelled as she ran towards the rest of the gang.

Jujy is a ten-year-old Asian girl who really loves playing softball. Her skills are average but when she put on her complete gear to play, her softball skills rocket beyond professional.

"Hey, Hunk, give me a push on this swing?" Dropz asked.

Dropz was a master at volleyball. Crowds of people would show up to her games to watch the eleven-year-old stomp out her competitors. When she slips on her sports gear, her level of skill is unexplainable. But she holds back her talent during those games for fear of what people might say.

"I'll push you," Buddafinger yelled as he scurried towards Dropz. "But hold on tight, because I'm gonna push you really high!"

Buddafinger is an eleven-year-old African-American who loves basketball. But when it comes time to play, he is usually the last one to get picked because of his clumsiness and inability to handle the ball. But little do some people know that when he puts on his basketball uniform, the ball becomes like magic in his hands. His skills become phenomenal.

"Thanks for waiting for me guys," Jujy says happily as she caught up with the gang.

"No problem," Hunk cheerfully replied.

Hunk is a twelve-year-old Indian-American and is passionate about football. He is a big kid, and he is the best when it comes to tearing turf on the field. He is especially a heavy hitter at tackling, but when he puts on his football gear he can play any position in the game.

Dropz jumped off the swing and suggested that they all walk to the ice cream parlor for ice cream.

"Great idea!" the gang exclaimed excitedly.

Hunk, however, told the gang that he wanted to go home to eat his mother's brownies.

"I'll catch up with y'all later," he said and quickly turned and ran toward his home. Three other friends named Tootsy, Twicks, and Pockits had to leave for home as well.

"I can't wait to fill my mouth full of delicious chocolate-flavored ice cream," Jujy said excitedly.

Buddafinger opened the door to the ice cream parlor, letting Twizz, Jujy, and Dropz go in first. They all ordered their ice cream and sat at the table to eat while telling stories to each other about the things that happened at school today.

Twizz got up from the table and headed towards the restroom. Twizz is an eleven-year-old Hispanic-American boy who loves soccer and hardly seems to be scared of anything. He's also very funny and always carries around a soccer ball, believing that he can become "one" with the ball. As people watch him practice on the soccer field, many would think that he does not belong in the sport. But it is a whole different story once he puts on his soccer clothes to play. His skills become superb and he becomes king of the field.

Buddafinger, Dropz and Jujy got up to wait for Twizz outside. But as they get to the exit, three big Out-of-Towners rushed through the door and yelled at the owner of the parlor to get them free ice cream before they beat him up.

Frightened, the store owner quickly filled three bowls with ice cream.

"Okay, here you go. Just please don't hurt me!"

One of the Out-of-Towners turned and saw Dropz holding a cup of ice cream. He walked over slowly, growled at her, showing his yellow teeth, and snatched the cup out of her hands.

"That is mines now," he yelled at her.

Twizz, heard all the commotion from inside the restroom and slowly opened the door to see what was going on. When he saw the three hoodlums, he quietly closed the door, ran into a stall, and put on his soccer clothes.

In less than a moment, the bathroom door swung open, and Twizz walked out in full soccer gear with his soccer ball in his hands.

"Give the ice cream back to my friend," Twizz demanded.

The Out-of-Towners laughed out loud.

"Little boy, who do you think you're talking to?" Don't you see how big we are? We'll crush you like a bug!"

One of the Out-of-Towners began to run towards Twizz. Twizz dropped his ball. But before it hit the floor, he gave it a hard thunder-sounding kick. The walls began to vibrate as the ball powerfully shoots through the air towards its target. All of a sudden, a sonic boom shattered the windows of the ice cream parlor and the soccer ball hit the Out-of-Towner square on the head and knocked him out cold.

The ball quickly returned into the hands of Twizz while the other two Out-of-Towners' jaws dropped open as they looked down on their friend in shock.

"Boyeeee, you're gonna pay for that!" one of the two conscious Out-of-Towners yelled. He grabbed an ice cream scooper and hesitantly walked towards Twizz.

Twizz dropped the soccer ball and placed his foot on top of it. The Out-of-Towner moved in closer as he lifted the ice cream scooper and charged towards Twizz, screaming at the top of his lungs.

Twizz smiled. Just as he shifted the ball with his foot a little to the right, Jujy quietly walked out of the bathroom in full softball gear.

The Out-of-Towner tried to swing the scooper at Twizz but was quickly stopped as a softball hit him in the face. He fell over onto his stomach, gasping for air from the hard hit.

The last Out Of Towner took a big gulp. He ran out the door, popped the trunk of a car, and got a bat. He marched back into the parlor.

"You two are in big trouble now," he threatened.

But Jujy pulled another ball out of her backpack.

"You picked the wrong place, pal. See if you can hit this." Jujy wound up the ball for a fast pitch. She released the ball and another sonic boom was heard (it was said) from a few blocks away.

The softball hit the last Out-of-Towner in the head and knocked him out cold.

The owner of the parlor quickly grabbed the phone and called the police. The police arrived and placed all three of the Out-of-Towners in handcuffs and placed them in the police car. "Wow, you kids have done a good job here!" the Chief of police congratulated them.
   "Thanks," the gang replied in unison.
   "That was very wild!" Buddafinger said intensely. They all gave a high five to each other and went their separate ways.

Two of the Out-of-Towners cried as they were put into jail awaiting to see the judge. The Out-of-Towner who wasn't crying paced the floor.

"Come on... get it together! We're going to break out of here."

After a few minutes of planning, one of them began yelling.

"Help! Help, officer! I need some help! My friend fainted and needs medical attention!"

The police officer opened the jail door and the Out-of-Towners quickly grabbed him, threw him down to the ground, and locked the door behind them. They ran out of the police station and stole a car for a fast getaway.

"Now let's go find those kids and punish them," one of them angrily said.

The next day, the Sport Kids gang gathered at the park to hang out. Buddafinger snapped his fingers and said, "Did y'all hear that the Out-of-Towners escaped from jail?"

Hunk looked at Buddafinger.

"Who are the Out-of-Towners?" he asked

Dropz abruptly cut in and explained.

"They are these three big boys who are triplets and they are very mean. I would have called them The Three Hippo Gang because they each are practically as big as a hippopotamus."

Jujy chimed in.

"We ran into them at the ice cream parlor, and they tried to rob the place. But we kicked their butts and they went to jail."

Hunk's eyes got wide.

"Oh, wow! I wish I could have been there. I would have taken them out with my pinkie finger."

The gang started laughing. Hunk was the only one not laughing.

"Well, if they have escaped, wouldn't they come looking for you?" he asked Jujy.

"Well, if they do, then I would show them a thing or two," Tootsy exclaimed.

Tootsy is an eleven-year-old African-American girl who is passionate about tennis, and her dream is to become a professional tennis player. She trains hard every day on the tennis courts but isn't quite as good at the game. But when she puts on her tennis gear, her skills are to be reckoned with.

As the Sport Kids laughed and talked about the trouble at the parlor, a massive black shadow slowly rose over them.

"And what exactly would you do to us?" one of the Out-of-Towers angrily asked Tootsy.

The Sports Kids stood there paralyzed in fear at the sheer size of these big guys.

"You messed up our plan to rob the ice cream parlor, and now we're going to make you pay."

The Sports Kids quickly dispersed to find places to put on their sports gear. Hunk forgot to bring his football gear, so he started running home to get it.

"I'll be back!" he yelled to his friends.

Buddafinger was in full basketball gear. He stood in front of the Out-of-Towers.

"You three are going back to jail!"

The Out-of-Towners laughed at him. Buddafinger grabbed his basketball and spun it really fast on top of his finger.

Suddenly, high winds began to kick up, twirling dust just as fast as the spinning ball and creating a small but powerful vortex.

The Out-of-Towners looked in amazement. Buddafinger repeated himself.

"I said, you three are going back to jail!"

Buddafinger flicked the ball towards them. The ball spun faster and the vortex grew bigger and bigger. The basketball spun around The Out-of-Towners, and the vortex lifted them off their feet and high into the air.

"Make it stop!" one of them yelled. Buddafinger stretched out his arm and the ball stopped spinning and returned back to him. The vortex disappears, and the powerful winds subsided. The Out-of-Towners fell to the ground.

"Ouch!" they painfully yelled. They immediately got off the ground and started running away

As they got to the sidewalk, one of them was suddenly hit hard by Hunk. The Out-of-Towner flew fifty feet and fell to the ground in a daze.

"Was that a train?" one of them asked.

Hunk got into a huddle position and yelled. "Blue 42, blue 42, down, set, hut!"

He took a few steps back and threw his football at such a high rate of speed that it cut through the air, making a high-pitched whistling sound like a bomb dropping from the sky.

One of the Out-of-Towners turned around and saw the football coming at him. He tried to catch it, but it slipped past his hands and hit him in the gut, picking him up off his feet sending him flying towards the police station.

"I will take down the last bad guy!" Twicks shouted.

Twicks was a ten-year-old Caucasian boy who had a passion to become a really good hockey player. During practice, he was always falling on the ice. But when he put on his complete hockey gear, he became the best of the best.

Twicks pulled out his hockey stick and slid down the pavement with his in-line skates. He swiftly glided towards the last of the Out-of-Towners. He skated in a zig-zag movement to confuse his enemy.

As Twicks closely approached the bad guy, he steadied his hockey stick closely, moving parallel to the ground. Twicks quickly swept the legs from underneath the Out-of-Towner, causing him to fall down hard to the ground and slide a few feet, creating a big plume of dust.

"Ouch! I give up!" the Out-of-Towner yelled.

The police arrived and took the Out-of-Towners back to jail. The Sports Kids gathered around the swing set and enjoyed some cool beverages as the sun set.

"I can't believe I forgot my football gear at home. I'm glad I live nearby," Hunk laughed.

"Hey, Hunk, you came back just in time. That hit was amazing!" Pockits praised him.

Pockits is an eleven-year-old Caucasian preppy kid who loves to golf. He was an amateur at the game and couldn't hit a beach ball with a club if it was in front of him. Whenever he put on his golfing clothes, however, his level of skills were unheard of.

"Well, we were all a team today, and that is what counts," Dropz said.

"Night is about to fall, and those street lights are about to come on. I've to get home," Dropz added.

The Sports Kids all said goodbye to each other and left for their homes with proud looks on their faces as they all thought about how they saved the world from three bad guys.

About the Author

Reginal ("Reggie") Jackson was born in Chandler, Arizona where he developed an interest in creative writing as a young child. In addition to mastering the slingshot, playing with his friends, and otherwise employing his vivid imagination in a number of daring adventures, Reggie's most enjoyable memory was writing storybooks for his classmates and reading them aloud to the class. The students were so captivated by Reggie's stories, that their attention would make him beam his signature smile.

Over thirty years later, Reggie has published his first book in a new children's series, *The Sports Kids: The Out-of-Towners.* In this series, Reggie relives a few adventures with his diverse group of friends, but with a twist.

Reggie is married and the father of four children. He lives in California where his family is involved in acting and enjoying the RV life.

Milton Keynes UK
Ingram Content Group UK Ltd.
UKHW021153070124
435543UK00010B/131